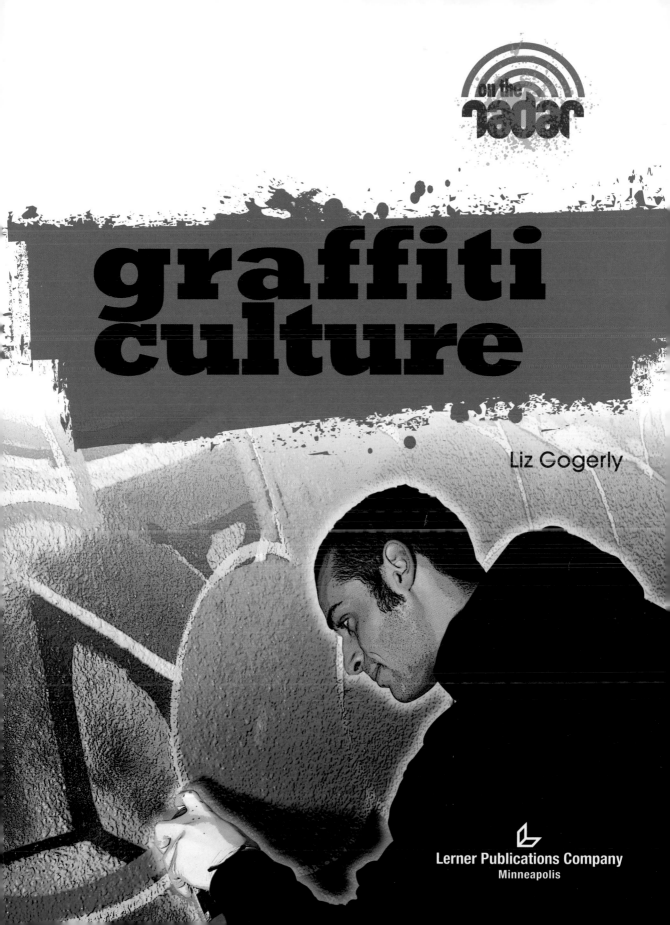

on the radar

graffiti culture

Liz Gogerly

Lerner Publications Company
Minneapolis

First American edition published in 2012 by Lerner Publishing Group, Inc. Published by arrangement with Wayland, a division of Hachette Children's Books

Lerner Publications Company
A division of Lerner Publishing Group, Inc.
241 First Avenue North
Minneapolis, MN U.S.A.

Website address: www.lernerbooks.com

Library of Congress Cataloging-in-Publication Data

Gogerly, Liz.
  Graffiti culture / by Liz Gogerly. — 1st American ed.
    p.   cm. — (On the radar: street style)
  Includes index.
  ISBN 978-0-7613-7767-2 (lib. bdg. : alk. paper)
    1. Graffiti—Juvenile literature. 2. Street art—Juvenile literature. I. Title.
  GT3912.G58 2012
  306.4—dc23   2011022305

Manufactured in the United States of America
1 – CG – 12/15/11

Acknowledgments: Corbis: Tim Mosenfender 16–17; Flickr: CopperKettle 18, Indieink 26–27, Thomas Locke Hobbs 22r, MrsMullerauh 28c, Los Cardinalos 23r, Bruce Turner 11; Hedz: 2c, 9bc, 9bl, 9c; iStockphoto: Reinhard Kaiser 10; Mosstika.com: Edina Tokodi/ Maxim Chelak 29b; Rex: Everett Collection 25, Sipa Press 31; Shutterstock: 7, 15r, Rob Ahrens 29l, BMCL 12, 2t, Diego Cervo 1, 4–5, 19b, Sam Cornwell 3br, 19t, 20t, Neale Cousland 23l, David Davis cover, Gary 718 14b, Hannamariah 8–9, Juhku 15t, Sergey Kamshylin 14c, L. Kragt Bakker 29t, Jon Le-Bon 19r, Blazej Maksym 9br, Pixel Memoirs 13, Roman Sigaev 28b, Stefanie Mohr 14br, Stefano Tiraboschi 2b, 22l; Wikipedia: 10t.

Main body text set in
Helvetica Neue LT Std 13/15.5.
Typeface provided by Adobe Systems.

cover stories

CONTENTS

thepeople

theart

thetalk

GRAFFITI

Graffiti can be a simple name tag or a work of art, but the very mention of the word *graffiti* can kick up a storm. Some people love it. Others think it's a crime. Some think it's about freedom of expression. Others think it ruins the urban environment. Graffiti causes people to disagree. But one thing is for certain—it plays a huge part in modern culture.

In the public eye

The word *graffiti* means "scratched," and it can be anything from words and markings to pictures and symbols. Most artists use cans of spray paint and chalk to leave their mark on walls and buildings. Graffiti is just about everywhere, from subway stations to tall skyscrapers. In the last few decades, graffiti art has even made its way into some of the most famous art galleries.

"Art in the Street" opened at the Museum of Contemporary Art in Los Angeles, California, in 2011. The exhibit shows off the works of U.S. and international graffiti artists. These include Shepard Fairey, Margaret Kilgallen, Banksy, and JR. Jean-Michel Basquiat's work is highlighted in a special gallery dedicated to 1980s artists.

Word on the street

Graffiti has its roots on the street. It gives ordinary people the power to deliver a message or share their thoughts in a visual way.

Painting for peace

Graffiti can also be a powerful tool for delivering messages of peace. Among the political messages on the Berlin Wall in Germany and the peace line gates in Northern Ireland were pleas for peace.

SPRAY-CAN SPEAK

Add graffiti cool to your street speak—follow the On the Radar guide!

aerosol
a can with a spray device that releases liquid, such as paint, from inside the can

back to back
graffiti that covers a wall from one side to the other

bombing
to thoroughly cover an area in graffiti

calligraphy
the art of producing beautiful or stylized handwriting and lettering

dirty
a layering style of creating graffiti

dressing up
to cover an area, such as a door or wall that has not been painted before

font
a specific style of lettering

freehand artist
an artist who paints without the guide of a device such as a stencil

king
an artist who is admired for his or her work and owns the most tags in a certain area

mark
to tag or write graffiti

paste-up
an extremely large sticker made by a graffiti artist and pasted onto a wall or other urban surface

piece
a term used by graffiti artists for a painting; short for masterpiece

run
the length of time a piece of graffiti remains on view to the public before it is removed or covered up by other graffiti

stencil
a sheet of material, such as paper or a card, that has a design cut out of it

sticker
a type of non-permanent graffiti. The artist adds anything (from a tag to more elaborate pieces) onto adhesive stickers.

tag
a graffiti artist's basic style of signature

3-D art
three-dimensional letters and images

throw-up
a graffiti term for an image that mostly consists of an outline and one fill-in color

top to bottom
a piece that extends from the top to the bottom of a train, a wall, or a building

GLOSSARY

Acropolis
an ancient site high on a hill in the Greek capital of Athens

Berlin Wall
the wall that divided West Germany from East Germany from 1961 to 1989

biodegradable
materials that rot away naturally

commercial graffiti artist
an artist who is paid to create graffiti art

commissioned
to be asked to create a piece of art on behalf of another person or organization

hip-hop
a style of music and dance that originated in the 1970s in New York

murals
pictures painted on walls

peace line gates, Northern Ireland
the series of separation barriers built in Northern Ireland to divide Catholic and Protestant areas

Pompeii
the ancient Roman town near Naples in Italy

race wars
fights between groups of people from different ethnic backgrounds

symbol
a picture that represents something else. For example, a dove is a symbol of peace.

underground
hidden or secret; not well known to many people

urban
relating to a city

vandalism
the malicious and intentional destruction of public or private property

STUART STYLES

Stuart is a leading commercial graffiti artist who runs his own urban art business called Hedz. As well as holding art workshops, Hedz creates amazing commercial artwork. On the Radar gets together with Stuart to discover more about the graffiti scene.

What do you love about doing graffiti?

Graffiti is the most invigorating and absorbing interest I have ever had. I love it because it's about freedom of expression. It connects with people, regardless of location, cultural background, or age group.

How do people get into the graffiti scene?

Graffiti is not an art form that you accidentally become involved with. In the past, many artists already knew one another because they were part of a network on the street. The network was hard for new artists to join. These days, Internet and social media coverage has made it much easier to connect with like-minded people.

What are your top tips for creating awesome artwork?

Researching your artistic ideas is my top tip for achieving amazing results. Most artists get lots of inspiration from the Internet. It's also important to share ideas with other artists. Once you have an idea, you've got to keep on practicing. When I first started, I sometimes had to repeat a painting thousands of times before I was happy!

Has creating graffiti ever gotten you into trouble with the police?

No, never. There is no value in creating art in an illegal environment. It can be dangerous and damaging to other people and their property.

Why do you think graffiti is good for our communities?

Graffiti is bright, exciting, and colorful—what better way is there to improve a neglected space within our communities? Graffiti art can also communicate some complex messages in a way that brings together people from different races, age groups, and social backgrounds.

Which products feature your graffiti designs?

We create designs for all kinds of products, from clothing to soccer nets. Our graffiti designs have also been used on TV commercials!

How can kids get involved with urban art?

There's never been a better time for aspiring urban artists to get into graffiti culture. I would recommend urban art workshops run in schools, colleges, and universities. Young people can gain access to urban culture in a safe and educational environment.

WRITINGS ON THE WALL

KILROY WAS HERE

Graffiti is hip, it's happening, and it has the edge. By its very nature, graffiti feels relevant to modern culture. But graffiti is nothing new. Throughout history people have scribbled on walls.

This ancient Roman graffiti can still be seen on a church in Rome, Italy.

Timeless graffiti

Ancient civilizations may not have had spray paints, but they shared modern society's need for self-expression. Examples of graffiti can be found on all kinds of ancient Greek, Roman, Mayan, and Viking sites. The Acropolis in Athens, Greece, is covered in ancient graffiti, including tags and ads. And the ancient Roman site at Pompeii, Italy, has a fascinating range of graffiti, from witty one-liners to confessions of love!

Paving the way

In sixteenth-century Italy, temporary graffiti grew in popularity when street painters, called I *madonnari*, created chalk portraits of the Madonna (Jesus's mother) or other religious scenes during holy festivals. In the nineteenth century, British street painters were called screevers. They used colored chalks to draw on sidewalks and lived off the donations they got from passersby.

World War doodles

During World War II (1939–1945), the message "Kilroy was here" appeared on walls and buildings everywhere. The message was combined with a drawing of Britain's "Mr. Chad." U.S. and British soldiers put the drawing and phrase wherever they were traveling or stationed during the war.

Hip-hop and happening!

In the late 1970s, graffiti exploded onto the urban street art scene. In New York, rival street gangs used graffiti to mark their territory and competed to create the most eye-catching art. The same gangs were into hip-hop music. Very soon hip-hop became the sound track for graffiti art. And graffiti became the signature of hip-hop. It was a marriage made on the streets.

Street to gallery

African American graffiti artist Jean-Michel Basquiat made the leap from the street to the gallery with his art in the 1980s. By the 2000s, graffiti art was no longer out of place in cool art galleries. Graffiti artists such as Shepard Fairey, Blu, and Banksy are famous all over the world. And artists such as Julian Beever and DAIM have taken graffiti to a whole new level with their amazing 3-D chalk pavement art.

Many of Shepard Fairey's works deliver a political message.

BANKSY

International man of mystery

Some people believe this classic Banksy piece is a political statement. The maid is said to be sweeping Britain's social problems under a curtain.

Underground scene

Banksy first got into graffiti in the 1990s on the streets of Bristol, England. In the early days, he was a freehand artist, but he took up stenciling because it was much quicker. Under cover of darkness, the stealthy stencil artist created funny scenes. Favorite subjects included police officers, rats, and children. Banksy used these images to get across his mistrust of the law.

Britain's number one graffiti artist

By the early 2000s, Banksy was Britain's number one graffiti artist. Nobody knew who he was, but more people knew about his art. Spotting "Banksies" on the streets of Bristol; London, England; and New York was as much a cultural exercise as visiting an art gallery. In 2002 Banksy got a taste of international fame with his first exhibition in Los Angeles, California. He also did the cover artwork for the band Blur's album *Think Tank*. Later that year, he took part with Dmote and Shepard Fairey in the Semi-Permanent Graffiti & Street Art Exhibition in Sydney, Australia.

The aloof spoof

Banksy has also been behind a series of art pranks. In 2004 he produced wads of phony money with "Banksy of England" on them. In 2005 he planted a fake cave painting at the British Museum in London. The painting looked real except it showed an early human hunting with a shopping cart!

Who is Banksy?

Banksy is among the most famous graffiti artists in the world. But the big question is, who is he? Nobody knows for sure. Like many graffiti artists, Banksy keeps his identity a secret. Most graffiti is illegal, so it pays to stay underground. And being a man of mystery seems to just add more to his street appeal!

Career highlights

2008 over three days, Banksy hosted "The Cans Festival" in Leake Street, London. Graffiti artists from all over the globe brought color to an abandoned part of the city.

2009 Banksy's Summer Show opened at Bristol's City Museum and Art Gallery. With over 100 pieces, it was his biggest exhibition to date.

2010 produced his first film called *Exit through the Gift Shop*

ART OR VANDALISM?

Urban artists believe that graffiti art is all about freedom of expression. They say:

1. Self-expression and freedom to protest is a basic human right. Graffiti is a nonviolent form of protest or political expression.
2. Urban landscapes can be transformed for the better! Graffiti brightens up rundown areas and decaying buildings.
3. It is a true art form that should be celebrated rather than condemned. These days, graffiti can be seen in art galleries, on designer clothes and accessories, and on music labels.
4. We can benefit from graffiti. Many community art projects bring people together and give young people a chance to express themselves.
5. Some graffiti artists use chalk, water, or other non-permanent methods for their work. Where is the harm in that?

AGAINST

Opponents of graffiti think it is a form of vandalism that ruins the urban environment. They say:

1. Graffiti is illegal, and the people who carry it out are trespassing. Not only are graffiti artists breaking the law, they are also making places look ugly.

2. Some artists use bad language or express views that can be offensive to the public. Sometimes the images can be rude or offensive too.

3. It costs millions to remove graffiti from urban areas. This money could be spent more effectively on making cities better places to live.

4. Graffiti is bad for business. Shops and other businesses that are covered in graffiti may lose customers because they think the shops look neglected.

5. Graffiti sends out a message that an area is crime ridden and therefore frightens people away.

RIGHT OR WRONG?

Some people view graffiti as art. Others think it is a crime against society. Graffiti remains against the law in most places. Some authorities compromise by creating graffiti zones, where artists are allowed to spray. Others give prison sentences for known offenders. Right or wrong, graffiti art remains a hotly debated topic!

M.I.A.

THE STATS

Name: Mathangi "Maya" Arulpragasam
Stage name: M.I.A.
Born: July 18, 1975
Place of birth: London, England
Nationality: British
Job: Rapper, singer, songwriter, record producer, graffiti artist

Starting out

Maya was born in London, but her parents came from Sri Lanka in South Asia. When she was six months old, her parents moved back to Sri Lanka. The family then stayed in this war-torn country for the next nine years. As a political activist, Maya's father was rarely around. In 1986 Maya's mother returned to London with her children.

Spray-paint inspiration

In 2001 Maya wowed the crowds at her first public art exhibition in London. All the influences of her early life were laid bare in a series of vibrant spray-paint and stencil canvases. The war scenes from her childhood were reflected in the graffiti-style art. Although she looked set to have a successful art career, she decided instead to focus on music.

Film, fashion, and fascinating rap

As a teenager, Maya mixed with other South Asian children in East London. In her early twenties, she earned a degree in fine art, film, and video at London's Central Saint Martins College of Art and Design. She shared an apartment with Justine Frischmann, frontwoman of the band Elastica. Justine commissioned Maya to create the cover of Elastica's album *The Menace* (2000).

Prize-winning artist

These days, Maya is an award-winning rapper and recording artist. In 2004 she broke through with singles "Galang" and "Sunshowers." Since then she has been nominated for British and U.S. music awards. Meanwhile, her background in graffiti gives her live shows, fashion, and music artwork an unique edge. Daring and outspoken, Maya is one of the most exciting artists of recent times and a political voice to be reckoned with.

PERMANENT STYLE

Whether graffiti is covering a wall back to back or dressing up a door, some graffiti artists want their work to last. Look out for these permanent styles.

Etching

This style of graffiti can leave permanent scars! Also known as scratchiti, this style requires the artist to use a sharp object such as a stone to scratch, or etch, into a material.

Tagging

The tag is the simplest and most common type of graffiti. It is the graffiti artist's signature or nickname as a design. Each artist develops his or her own style and usually sticks to one range of color.

etching

Stenciling

Graffiti artists often work against the clock and under cover of darkness. Stencil graffiti is one way to pull off some nifty pieces in double-quick time. The same piece of art can be repeated over and over with minimal effort!

Spray painting

Spray-paint art is long lasting and eye catching. Graffiti opponents view spray-paint art as public enemy number one because it is so hard to remove.

tagging

stenciling

HEY BANKSY WHY DONT YOU RETURN MY EMAILS

spray painting

GRAFFITI TAG

Your tag should stand out in a crowd, so it is important to get it just right. You want something cool and unforgettable—a tag that's guaranteed to turn heads!

You will need:

- paper • pencils • marker pens
- imagination and creativity

1 Think about the tag you want to create. What do you want it to say about you?

2 Write your tag in large letters on a piece of paper. Play around with the size and shape of the letters.

3 Experiment with the thickness of the lines, and add shading to give the letters a 3-D effect.

4

Get out your marker pens and fill in the letters. Be as creative as you can with the colors.

Got it?

Check out the finished article. Would you be proud to leave this mark on your personal belongings? Keep practicing and collect your tags in your own graffiti design scrapbook.

5

Add detail to your tag—but try not to get too carried away because sometimes the simplest tags are the best!

PASSPORT TO PAINT

The world is the graffiti artist's canvas. Any urban space is an inviting place for artists to make their mark. Throughout the world, urban artists are hard at work.

The graffiti capital, New York *(left)*, is famous for its colorful urban art. The stairways of São Paulo, Brazil *(above)*, are covered with murals.

The graffiti capital

New York City without graffiti? Unthinkable! Like it or not, the city is famous for its edgy, creative, and in-your-face messages. They appear on buildings, on isolated subway walls, and on vehicles of all kinds. The famous underground film *Wild Style* (1983) captured the hip-hop and graffiti scene in the city of their birth. Check it out on DVD!

The streets of São Paulo

Anyone visiting São Paulo, Brazil, should take one of the graffiti tours. The buzzing South American city is a hotbed of cool graffiti. At every turn are colorful murals, exciting lettering, and amazing pieces. Some people liken the scene in São Paulo to New York in the 1970s. The city certainly shares some of New York's problems, such as poverty, unemployment, and urban decay—all of which are expressed in its graffiti art.

Much of the stencil graffiti in Melbourne, Australia *(below left)*, is designed to make a political or social statement. A graffiti gangster in Paris, France, wears hip-hop jewelry emblazoned with the city's name *(below right)*.

Aussie art

Some people call Melbourne, Australia, the stencil capital of the world, because its sidewalks and buildings feature some of the best stencil graffiti you will find. One of the stars of the local scene is a female graffiti artist named Vexta. She stands out in a mainly male graffiti world. As well as stencil art, she's famous for her stickers and paste-ups.

Art attack in Paris

France has legal graffiti sites all over the country with some exciting spaces within its parks in Paris. However, graffiti is a product of the streets and probably always will be. In fact, an anonymous artist has been at large in Paris since 2010. In response to the French government's ban of the Muslim veil in public, this artist adds veils to the fashion advertisements on giant billboards across the city!

DAVID CHOE

King of the dirty style

Art therapy

David Choe grew up in the tough neighborhood of Koreatown in Los Angeles. His parents were Korean immigrants who had their own property business. As a boy, David was interested in superheroes and *Star Wars* movies. Then, at the age of 14, he discovered graffiti. Over time, this art form helped David deal with the difficulties of growing up in a troubled society where crime and race wars were common.

On the road

When he finished high school, David traveled in the United States, Europe, and Africa. After two years on the road, he enrolled at the California College of the Arts. While there, he developed a method of painting with almost any medium, from spray paint and crayons to oil—all layered on top of one another. David called this approach to graffiti art his dirty style, and it has become his signature.

Doing time

In 2003 David served a three-month jail sentence for a minor offense. During this time, he experimented with his art and began to use different and unusual materials such as soy sauce and even blood! This spell in prison made David think differently about his life. When he returned to Los Angeles, he found peace in his work. David then began to exhibit his art and accepted commissions. In 2004 he created the cover for the Jay-Z and Linkin Park CD *Collision Course*. In 2005 and 2007, David created artwork for the Facebook offices.

Barack and beyond

In 2008 David hit the big time when he created his *Hope* piece for then-presidential candidate Barack Obama. The same year, David became a star of his own TV travel show *Thumbs Up!* It trails the graffiti artist on his adventures around the world. David and his dirty art made such fascinating viewing that the program has run for three series. Despite being a hugely successful commercial artist and muralist, David is still drawn to his first love—street graffiti.

Career highlights

1999 self-published the cult classic graphic novel *Slow Jams*

2007 commissioned to create the sets for the comedy drama *Juno*

2011 Mark Zuckerberg asked David to create a new painting for the Facebook offices in California

THE STATS

Name: David Choe
Born: April 22, 1976
Place of birth:
Los Angeles, California
Personal life: Likes to
explore all artistic mediums
and to travel
Job: Graffiti artist, painter,
graphic novelist

David paints with many types of media, from ink to oil, using one on top of the other to create layers of images.

SHADOW GRAFFITI

Most public graffiti is illegal. However, some local authorities or property owners don't mind chalk graffiti. Chalk washes away easily, so many people don't see it as a problem. Chalk can be used to create stunning shadow graffiti. This art form is not as common as paint graffiti, but the idea is catching on.

Essential technique

• Sunshine or a streetlight is a must to create strong shadows.

• Be quick on the draw. Shadows move quickly and so should the artist!

HOW IT'S DONE

1. The artist finds a suitable subject. Beginners often go for something that has a strong outline and is easy to copy, such as a street sign or a tree.
2. Using light strokes, the artist chalks around the shadow in white.
3. Once happy with the outline of the shadow, the artist colors it in using black chalk.

Why do it?

Shadow graffiti creates a stunning image that attracts attention from passersby. People question whether the shadow is real or imaginary. The ultimate goal of any art piece is to make people stop and stare, and shadow graffiti does just that!

TEMPORARY ART

chalk

reverse graffiti

water calligraphy

As governments around the world have cracked down on graffiti, some artists have turned to non-permanent forms of graffiti. They have ditched the spray-paint cans and marker pens to experiment with chalk, water, stickers, grass, and even moss!

Chalk talk

Chalk is biodegradable and washes away in the rain. For this reason, local authorities rarely prosecute anyone caught using chalk, so young artists often use it for drawing tags. Chalk can also be blended to create different shades. This makes for magnificent examples of 3-D art.

Clean graffiti

Reverse graffiti is also known as clean tagging, clean graffiti, dust tagging, or grime writing. All that is required is a dirty surface—such as a window, a vehicle, or a wall. The artist writes a message or draws a design using a fingertip in the dirt. Artists can also clean an area using pressure washing.

Writing in water

All that a water calligraphy artist needs is a large brush, a bucket of water, and a sidewalk on which to write. A message is daubed onto the sidewalks using the brush and water, and within minutes, the words fade away. It is simple but magical to watch.

Sticker bombing

The graffiti artist writes or prints a tag, a message, or a design onto a sticker. The stickers can then be stuck anywhere, from walls and streetlamps to billboards and schoolbags.

Going green

Natural products such as moss and grass can be used to create the ultimate green graffiti. Artists simply stick the moss or the grass to a wall using biodegradable products. They use this technique to create different words and images.

sticker bombing

moss art

Actress AnnaLynne McCord adds street to her style with a fluorescent graffiti handbag.

DESIGNER GRAFFITI

A bond between graffiti and fashion has developed. But when did this relationship begin? And where will it end?

Spray-paint success

In the 1980s, graffiti grabbed the limelight. The craze for changing the urban landscape took off. It was not long before bold lettering and vibrant graffiti pieces were brightening up clothes. First came big T-shirts decorated with graffiti. For example, designer Marc Ecko set up his fashion company in 1993 with just six T-shirts and a can of spray paint. He is now head of the billion-dollar fashion and lifestyle company Marc Ecko Enterprises.

Artists at the ready

New York graffiti artist Erni Vales became involved in the luxury end of fashion when he designed a range of graffiti handbags. Likewise, Claw Money's claw logo is actually the throw-up she used to paint on walls. These days, it decorates T-shirts, shoes, bags, and baby clothes.

Ultimate makeover

Fashion designer Marc Jacobs was looking for a way to revamp Louis Vuitton's traditional handbags and luggage. Jacobs remembers coming up with the idea of using the work of graffiti artist Stephen Sprouse. "The idea of Stephen Sprouse's graffiti on canvas—defacing something respected and venerable—was very bold. But it also felt right."

Yarn bombing

Among the newest graffiti forms is yarn bombing. Knitters have covered statues, tree trunks, cars, and buses with colorful yarn. They record themselves doing it and post the results on social network sites. Perhaps the most impressive effort was artist Olek's covering of *Charging Bull*, the huge statue near Wall Street in New York City.

Urban art fever

In 2011 fashion label Moschino treated us to the graffiti jacket for men and the graffiti summer dress for women. But the use of urban art is not restricted to designer labels. Ordinary chain stores offer graffiti clothing at reasonable prices. Graffiti fever, it seems, is here to stay.

FOR MORE INFO

Books

Banksy. *Wall and Peace*. London: Random House, 2007. The mysterious graffiti artist shares some of his favorite works in this book.

Felisbet, Eric. *Graffiti New York*. New York: Harry N. Abrams, 2009. This book details the origins and development of graffiti in New York.

Ganz, Nicholas. *Graffiti Women*. New York: Harry N. Abrams, 2006. Learn more about the contribution of women artists to graffiti culture.

Gogerly, Liz. *Street Dance*. Minneapolis: Lerner Publications Company, 2012. Learn more about hip-hop and street dance, which evolved alongside graffiti art.

Websites

Legal Walls U.S.A.
http://www.antidesigns.com/
legalgrafwalls.php
This site locates legal graffiti walls in the United States.

Off the Wall Graffiti
http://offthewallgraffiti.com
This site is the home of a nonprofit graffiti foundation. It has videos, highlights featured graffiti artists, and offers opportunities for creating legal graffiti.

@149 Street
htttp://www.at149st.com
This website documents the graffiti scene in New York's subway system.

INDEX